Now I Know™
A Calf Grows Up

by MELVIN AND GILDA BERGER

SCHOLASTIC INC.

New York   Toronto   London   Auckland   Sydney
Mexico City   New Delhi   Hong Kong   Buenos Aires

ISBN-13: 978-0-439-02529-4
ISBN-10: 0-439-02529-X

12 11 10 9 8 7 6 5 4 3 2 1   8 9 10 11 12 13/0

Printed in the U.S.A.
First Printing, March 2008

A calf is a baby animal.

Its mother is called a cow.

Its father is called a bull.

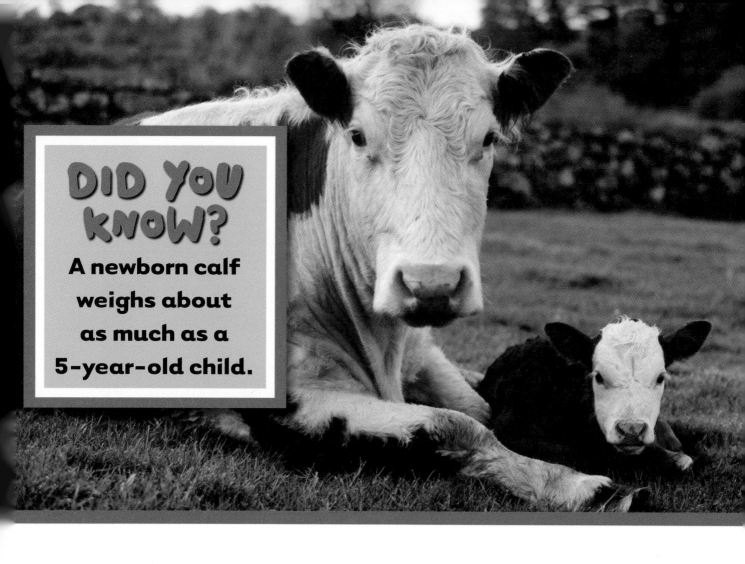

DID YOU KNOW?
A newborn calf weighs about as much as a 5-year-old child.

A calf is usually born in the spring.

The mother cow licks her calf clean.

The newborn calf cannot
stand at first.

It slowly gets up on its four legs.

ZOOM!

DID YOU KNOW?
A calf drinks more than a
gallon of milk a day.

Now the baby can
drink its mother's milk.

10

Sometimes the farmer
feeds the calf milk.

A calf drinks its mother's
milk for one year.

The calf stays close to its mother.

The calf has a long tail
just like its mother.

Swish! Get away, bugs!

A calf can be white, brown, black—

or a mix of colors.

The calf goes to pasture
with its mother.

ZOOM!

Mother and calf eat grass.

19

Sometimes the farmer
feeds the calves.

The calves eat hay or grain.

Calves can't answer to their names like dogs or horses can.

A calf grows fast.

A two-year-old calf is as
big as its mother.

Look! The calf is now a mother.

The new mother cares for
her calf.

The young cow feeds her calf milk.

The farmer takes some
of the milk, too.

Some cows and calves
stay on the farm.

Others graze on large ranches.

Round 'em up!

MOO-O-O!

GLOSSARY

Bull: A grown-up male calf.

Calf: A young cow or bull.

Cow: A grown-up female calf.

Farm: Land used for raising animals or growing crops.

Farmer: A person who raises animals and grows crops.

Gallon: A large unit of liquid equal to four quarts.

Grain: The tiny seeds of cereal plants, such as wheat, corn, or rice.

Graze: To eat grass growing in a field.

Hay: Grass that is cut and dried, and fed to animals.

Milk: The white liquid made by cows and other female mammals to feed their young.

Newborn: An animal that is just born.

Pasture: Land where grass grows and animals feed.

Ranches: Large farms for calves, cows, bulls, sheep, or horses.